Guess What!

Workbook 4

with Digital Pack

American English

Lynne Marie Robertson

Series Editor: Lesley Koustaff

Shaftesbury Road, Cambridge CB2 8EA, United Kingdom

One Liberty Plaza, 20th Floor, New York, NY 10006, USA

477 Williamstown Road, Port Melbourne, VIC 3207, Australia

314–321, 3rd Floor, Plot 3, Splendor Forum, Jasola District Centre, New Delhi – 110025, India

103 Penang Road, #05–06/07, Visioncrest Commercial, Singapore 238467

Cambridge University Press & Assessment is a department of the University of Cambridge.

We share the University's mission to contribute to society through the pursuit of education, learning and research at the highest international levels of excellence.

www.cambridge.org
Information on this title: www.cambridge.org/9781009798754

First published 2016
Updated edition 2024

20 19 18 17 16 15 14 13 12 11 10 9 8 7 6 5 4 3

Printed in Poland by Opolgraf

A catalogue record for this publication is available from the British Library

ISBN 978-1-009-79875-4 Workbook with Digital Pack Level 4
ISBN 978-1-009-79860-0 Student's Book with eBook Level 4
ISBN 978-1-009-48442-8 Teacher's Book with Digital Pack Level 4
ISBN 978-1-107-54546-5 Flashcards Level 4

Additional resources for this publication at www.cambridge.org/guesswhatue

Cambridge University Press & Assessment has no responsibility for the persistence or accuracy of URLs for external or third-party internet websites referred to in this publication, and does not guarantee that any content on such websites is, or will remain, accurate or appropriate. Information regarding prices, travel timetables, and other factual information given in this work is correct at the time of first printing but Cambridge University Press & Assessment does not guarantee the accuracy of such information thereafter.

Contents

Welcome back!

1 **Look and write the number.**

curly hair	straight hair	fair hair	red hair	dark hair	glasses
☐	☐	☐	☐	☐	1

2 **Look and write the words.**

1 He has _____short_____ hair.

2 She has _____long_____ hair.

3 He has _____ hair.

4 She has _____ .

5 He has _____ hair.

6 She has _____ hair.

7 He has _____ .

8 She has _____ hair.

3 **Think** **Look at activity 2. Write the words.**

How are they the same?	How are they different?
1 He has _____curly_____ hair.	2 He has _____ hair.
She has _____curly_____ hair.	She has _____ hair.
3 He has _____ .	4 He has _____ hair.
She has _____ .	She has _____ hair.

My picture dictionary → Go to page 84: Find and write the new words.

4 Read and match.

1 She's tall. She has short straight hair. _b_

2 He's short. He has big glasses. ____

3 She's tall. She has long straight hair. ____

4 He's short. He has small glasses. ____

5 She's short. She has curly red hair. ____

5 Look and complete the questions and answers.

1 (Tim) What does ___he look like?___

_____ tall. _____

short fair hair and big glasses.

2 (Helen) What does _____?

_____ short. _____

short curly hair and small glasses.

3 (Simon) What does _____?

_____ short. _____

curly dark hair and small sunglasses.

4 (Laura) What does _____?

_____ tall. _____ straight red hair and big sunglasses.

Tim　　Helen　　Simon　　Laura

6 Write about a person in your family.

My ... has ... hair _____

_____

_____

Look and match. Then write the answers.

86 cm   ~~1 m, 23 cm~~   28 cm   1 m, 55 cm   64 cm

1   How tall is the boy? He's 1 meter, 23 centimeters.

2   How high is the chair? It's

3   How tall is the girl?

4   How tall is the rabbit?

5   How high is the guitar?

 Answer the questions.

1   How tall is your friend?

2   How tall is your mom/dad?

3   How tall are you?

4   How high is your chair?

Skills: *Writing*

9 **Read the paragraph and write the words.**

> dark   short   ~~1 m, 22 cm~~   movie theater   blue   playing   71 cm   bike

My friend's name is Paul. He's ¹ <u>1 m, 22 cm</u> tall. He has
² _____ ³ _____ hair. He likes
⁴ _____ soccer. He has a ⁵ _____
⁶ _____ . It's ⁷ _____ high. He likes going
to the ⁸ _____ on Saturdays.

10 (About Me) **Answer the questions.**

1 What's your friend's name?

My friend's name is _____

2 How tall is your friend?

_____

3 What does your friend look like?

_____

4 What sports does your friend like?

_____

5 What activities does your friend like doing?

_____

11 (About Me) **Write about your friend.**

My friend's _____

_____

_____

12 (About Me) **Think of a friend. Ask and answer with another friend.**

What does your friend look like?   She has fair hair and glasses.

Is it Mary?   Yes, it is!

Skills **7**

13 Read and match.

> 1 Let's register now!   3 ~~No, let's watch TV.~~
> 2 We all like adventures.   4 Do you want to help your local community?

a

What should we do this afternoon?

How about swimming?

_3_

b

I do! I do!

Anna! Sit down.

c

We're making a new Adventure Playground. Register online for the free app.

Exciting!
_____

d

What should we call our team?

How about the Adventurers? _____.

Good idea.

14 Look at activity 13. Circle the answers.

1 They want to _____ .
   a play in the rain   b go swimming   c (watch TV)

2 *Daisy does it!* is the name of _____ .
   a their friend   b their community   c a TV program

3 The TV program asks them to _____ .
   a make a new supermarket   b help their community
   c make a new school

4 They register to _____ .
   a get a free app   b watch TV   c sit down

5 The Adventurers is the name of _____ .
   a their team   b the local community   c the new playground

15 **Read and check the activities that show the value: get involved with your local community.**

1 help make a playground ✓

2 ride your bike ☐

3 pick up garbage ☐

4 go to school ☐

5 read a book ☐

6 clean the beach ☐

16 **Find and check the words that sound like *owl*.**

1
 a ✓
 b ✓
 c ☐

2
 a ☐
 b ☐
 c ☐

3
 a ☐
 b ☐
 c ☐

4
 a ☐
 b ☐
 c ☐

What **patterns** can you see?

1 Look and read. Circle the patterns you can see.

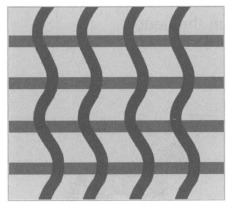

1 zigzags and wavy lines
(wavy lines and stripes)
stripes and zigzags

2 spots and stripes
wavy lines and spots
zigzags and spots

3 wavy lines and stripes
stripes and zigzags
zigzags and wavy lines

2 Read and draw.

1
Draw four green zigzags at the top.
Draw six red stripes under the zigzags.
Draw two purple spots under the stripes.

2
Draw a circle.
Draw nine blue spots in the circle.
Draw three orange stripes next to the circle.

3
Draw a big square.
Draw seven yellow stripes in the square.
Draw six black wavy lines between the stripes.

Evaluation

1 **Look and write the questions and answers. Then match.**

1 What does Sally
  __look__ __like__ ? ←

Raul

2 What does Herman
  _____ _____ ?

Sally

3 What does Macy
  _____ _____ ?

Herman

4 What does Raul
  _____ _____ ?

Macy

a _____ tall. _____
  _____ fair hair and
  sunglasses.

b _____ short. _____
  _____ long straight hair
  and small glasses.

c __She's__ tall. __She__
  __has__ curly red hair
  and sunglasses.

d _____ short. _____
  _____ short dark hair
  and big glasses.

2 (About Me) **Complete the sentences about this unit.**

1 I can talk about _____ .

2 I can write about _____ .

3 My favorite part is _____ .

3 Puzzle **Guess what it is.**

Hair that's not straight.
What is it? _____

Go to page 93 and write the answer.

1 Fun sports

1 Look and write the numbers.

☐ mountain biking   ☐ snowboarding   **1** sailing   ☐ fishing   ☐ skiing

☐ ice-skating   ☐ bowling   ☐ kayaking   ☐ skateboarding

2 Think Where do you do the sports? Look at activity 1 and write.

river/ocean	mountain	city/town
1 _sailing_	4 _____	7 _____
2 _____	5 _____	8 _____
3 _____	6 _____	9 _____

My picture dictionary → Go to page 85: Find and write the new words.

3 **Look and read. Then circle.**

1 He's / (He isn't) very good at kayaking.
3 He's / He isn't good at skateboarding.
5 She's / She isn't good at skiing.

2 She's / She isn't good at mountain biking.
4 He's / He isn't very good at ice-skating.

4 **Look and write the words.**

1

I'm not very good at skateboarding .

2

_____ good at ice-skating.

3

_____ very good at _____ .

4

_____

5 Complete the conversations.

Are you _good at bowling?_

Yes, __I am__ .

_____ good at ice-skating?

No, _____ .

_____ good at?

_____ good at playing the piano.

6 **Look and write.**

Ben	mountain biking ✗	guitar ✓	**Liz**	kayaking ✓	violin ✗

1 **Ben:** _____ _Are you_ _____ good at playing the violin? **Liz:** _____ _No, I'm not._ _____

2 **Liz:** _____ good at mountain biking?

Ben: _____

3 **Ben:** _____ good at?

Liz: _____ good at _____ .

4 **Liz:** _____ good at?

Ben: _____ good at _____ .

7 **Answer the questions.**

1 Are you good at music? _____

2 Are you good at skiing? _____

3 What are you good at? _____

4 What are you not very good at? _____

5 What do you want to be good at? _____

Skills: *Writing*

8 **Read and answer. Circle *yes* or *no*.**

Are you good at … ?

music	yes	no	making movies	yes	no
art	yes	no	playing Ping-Pong	yes	no
dancing	yes	no	gymnastics	yes	no
singing	yes	no	karate	yes	no
playing the piano	yes	no	playing the guitar	yes	no

9 **Ask three friends. Write their name and answers.**

What are you good at?   I'm good at singing.

Name:	Good at:
_____	_____
_____	_____
_____	_____

10 **Look at activities 8 and 9. Plan a talent show.**

Talent show!

Time: 6 o'clock
Place: gym

1. Heidi's good at singing. And she can dance.
2. Jim's good at playing the guitar.
3. Me – I'm good at making movies about karate.

Talent show!
Time: _____
Place: _____
1 _____
_____
2 _____
_____
3 _____
_____

11 Read and number in order.

a. Who wants to help paint the wall?

I do! I'm good at painting.

So are we, Anna! Let's all help.

b. It looks great. Good job!

It's me!

c. Wait and see, Anna.

Who are you painting, Lily?

d. Red hair and green eyes. Good!

Can I see?

Shh, Anna!

e. Welcome to Pinton Woods! I'm Daisy.

Hello. We're the Adventurers.

f. Thanks, Grandma!

We don't need this paint. Here you are.

1

12 Look at activity 11. Answer the questions.

1   Who gives paint to the children?   *Grandma*

2   What do the children help paint?   _____

3   Are the children good at painting?   _____

4   Who does Lily paint?   _____

5   Does Daisy like the wall painting?   _____

13 Look and check the picture that shows the value: allow others to work.

1

2

3

14 Find and check the words that sound like *coil*.

1 **a**
 ✓

b

c

2 **a**
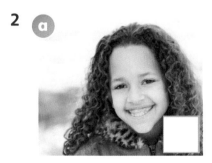

b

c

3 **a**

b
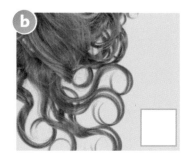

c

What kind of body movements can we make?

1 What body movements can you see? Circle the correct words.

1 stretch, bend, kick
kick, bend, stretch
~~bend, stretch, kick~~

2 turn, stretch, shake
shake, stretch, turn
bend, stretch, turn

3 shake, bend, kick
kick, shake, turn
shake, turn, bend

2 Complete the sentences with body movements.

1 She can _b_ _e_ _n_ _d_ her body.

2 He can _ _ _ _ his head.

3 She wants to _ _ _ _ _ _ _ her legs.

4 Let's _ _ _ _ _ the musical instruments.

5 He can _ _ _ _ the ball.

Evaluation

 Look and write.

1

What are you good at?
I'm good at making models.

2

What are you good at?
_____ good at skiing.

3

_____

_____

4

_____

_____

5

_____

_____

 Complete the sentences about this unit.

1 I can talk about _____ .

2 I can write about _____ .

3 My favorite part is _____ .

  Guess what it is.

You need water and wind to do this sport. What is it? _____

Go to page 93 and write the answer.

19

2 Around town

1 **Look and number the picture.**

1 ~~shopping mall~~
2 subway station
3 bus station
4 restaurant
5 square
6 bank

2 (Think) **Read and match. Then write the words.**

1 It means stop and go. It's red, yellow, and green.
2 It's black and white. It's not an animal.
3 I can eat here.
4 I can sleep here.
5 I can see art here.

museum
restaurant
~~traffic light~~
hotel
crosswalk

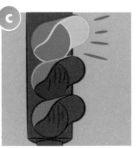

_____   _____   traffic light   _____   _____

My picture dictionary → Go to page 86: Find and write the new words.

3 **Look and circle the correct answers.**

1 Where's the restaurant?
   It's _____ the hotel.
   a above   **b** across from   **c** below

2 Where's the museum?
   It's _____ the traffic light.
   a below   **b** across from   **c** far from

3 Where's the subway station?
   It's _____ the hotel.
   a below   **b** next to   **c** above

4 Where's the shopping mall?
   It's _____ the museum.
   a across from   **b** next to   **c** far from

5 Where's the bank?
   It's _____ the crosswalk.
   a close to   **b** below   **c** far from

 Look at activity 3. Complete the questions and answers.

1 _Where's_ the train?
   It's _next to_ the hotel.

2 _____ the helicopter?
   It's _____ the bank.

3 _____ the car?
   It's _____ the shopping mall.

4 _____ the train?
   It's _____ the plane.

5 _____ the traffic light?
   It's _____ the crosswalk.

5 (Think) **Read and draw lines. Then answer the questions.**

1 Start at the subway station.
Turn right. Turn left at the traffic
light. It's on the left. Where are you?

_____ hotel _____

2 Start at the restaurant.
Turn right. Turn left. It's
on the right, across from
the hotel. Where are you?

_____

3 Start at the park. Cross the first
crosswalk. Turn left. Go straight ahead.
It's on the right, across from the square.
Where are you?

_____

4 Start at the shopping mall.
Turn right and go straight
ahead. Turn left at the
crosswalk. Go straight ahead.
Turn right at the crosswalk.
Stop. Where are you?

_____

5 Start at the square. Turn right.
Turn left. Go straight ahead. Turn left
after the museum. Stop. Where are you?

_____

 Look at activity 5. Write the directions.

1 Where's the museum? Start at the bank. _Turn_ _____

_____

2 Where's the bus station? Start at the square. _____

_____

3 Where's the park? Start at the movie theater. _____

_____

Skills: *Writing*

7 Read the paragraph and write the words.

museum   restaurants   ~~square~~   shopping mall   station

My Favorite City

My favorite city is Tokyo, in Japan. You can see a statue of a famous dog, Hachiko, in a ¹ _____ *square* _____ . I like eating at cafés and ² _____ there, too. I also like going shopping in Harajuku. You can see lots of beautiful clothes at the ³ _____ . Yoyogi Park is next to the subway ⁴ _____ . You can see bands playing music. The art ⁵ _____ is across from the park on the left. You can see old Japanese art there.

8 **Answer the questions.**

1   What's your favorite city?

My favorite city is _____

2   What do you like doing there?

_____

3   Where do you like going?

_____

4   What can you see there?

_____

9 **Write about your favorite city or town.**

My favorite city is _____

_____

_____

_____

10 **Ask and answer with a friend.**

What's your favorite city?   My favorite city is Madrid.

11 Read and match.

1 Stop at the traffic lights. 2 Turn left at the museum and go straight ahead.
3 Can we have the net, please? 4 ~~I know. Follow me.~~

a Look at this! A net!

Soccer competition Harton Park
How many goals can you score?

Where's Harton?

_4_

b Be careful, everyone.

_____

Yes, OK.

to Harton

c Excuse me. How do you get to the park?

Thanks.

MUSEUM

_____

d _____

It's for the Adventure Playground.

OK!

12 Look at activity 11. Write yes or no.

1 The museum is close to the park. _yes_

2 Tom knows where Harton is. _____

3 It's safe to stop at the traffic lights. _____

4 They turn right at the museum. _____

5 They get a net at the park. _____

13 **Look and check the pictures that show the value: cycle safely.**

14 **Color the words that sound like *surf*. Then answer the question.**

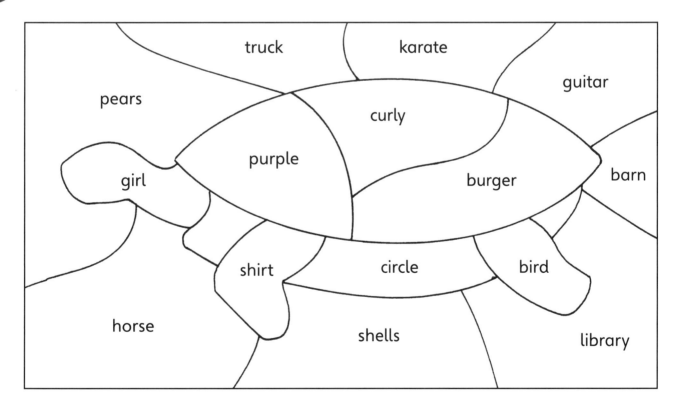

What is it? _____

What 3-D shapes can you see?

1 **Read and match.**

1 There are four cylinders. `b`

2 There's a big cube and a small pyramid.

3 There's a big sphere and four small spheres.

4 There are four small cones and a pyramid.

5 There are four small cones and a cube.

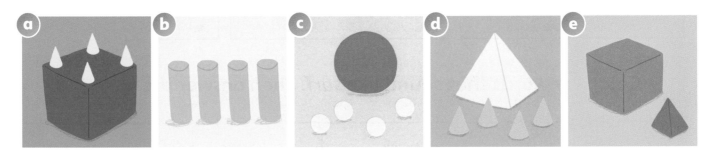

2 **Draw the 3-D shapes.**

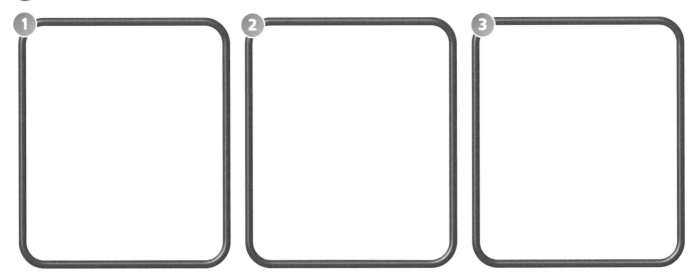

1 Draw a museum. It's a cube. It has two cone shapes and five cylinders.
2 Draw an subway station. It's a cylinder. It has eight spheres and three pyramids.
3 Draw a hotel. It's a pyramid. It has a cube at the front and a sphere on top.

Evaluation

1 **Look and complete the questions and answers.**

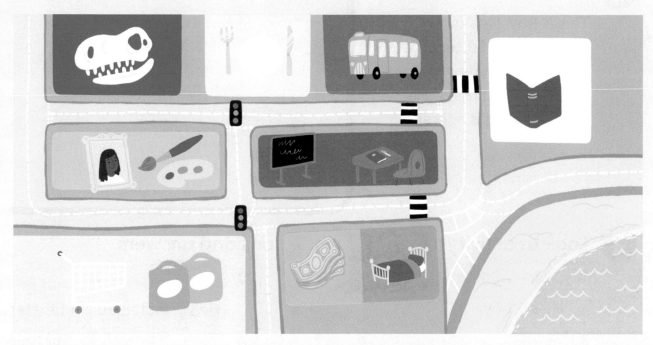

1 Where's the bank?

It's <u>next to</u> the hotel.

2 Where's the art gallery?

It's _____ the museum.

3 Where's the shopping mall?

It's _____ the book store.

4 Where's the restaurant?

It's _____ the bus station.

2 (About Me) **Complete the sentences about this unit.**

1 I can talk about _____ .

2 I can write about _____ .

3 My favorite part is _____ .

3 (Puzzle) **Guess what it is.**

You stop when it's red. You go when it's green. What is it?

_____

Go to page 93 and write the answer.

27

Review Units 1 and 2

1 **Read and draw.**

This is Ray. He's a boy. He's 1 meter, 50 centimeters tall. He has curly brown hair. He has glasses. His favorite sport is soccer.

2 **Look at activity 1. Write the questions and answers.**

1 _Is Ray a boy or a girl?_

He's a boy.

2 _____

He's 1 meter, 50 centimeters.

3 _____ ?

He's tall. He has curly hair.

4 _____ fair hair?

No, _____ .

5 _____ glasses?

Yes, _____ .

6 _____ soccer?

Yes, _____ .

3 **Look and write.**

1 Me

I'm _not very good at ice-skating_ .

2 Me

_____ good at _____ .

3 Henri

He's _____ .

4 Lori

She's _____ .

4 (About Me) **Look at activity 3 and write about you.**

1 I'm _____ at ice-skating. **2** I'm _____ at bowling.

3 _____ **4** _____

5 **Look and complete the questions and answers. Then match.**

| 3 | _Are you good at singing?_ |

No, _____ .

[ ] _____ good at playing the piano?

Yes, _____ .

[ ] _____ good at playing the recorder?

Yes, _____ .

[ ] _____ good at playing the guitar?

No, _____ .

6 (Think) **Do the puzzle. Then use the letters in the circles to answer the question.**

Across →

1 2 4 5

6 9 10

Down ↓

3 7 8

1 b u s s t a t i o n

Which letter of the alphabet has lots of w _ _ _ _ ? The "_____" (sea).

3 At work

1 (Think) **Write the words. Then check ✓ the one that doesn't belong.**

1

 ✓

actor   doctor   nurse

2

3

4

actor
~~actor~~
actor
artist
bus driver
businessman
businesswoman
~~doctor~~
~~nurse~~
pilot
singer
singer
vet

2 (Think) **Look at activity 1. Write the words.**

Where do they work?		
in a hospital	**in an office**	**in a theater**
doctor		

My picture dictionary → Go to page 87: Find and write the new words.

3 **Put the words in order. Then match.**

1 do / your / What / does / dad / ?

What does your dad do?

a She's / businesswoman / a / .

_____

2 aunt / does / do / your / What / ?

_____

b vet / a / He's / .

_____

3 do / your / does / uncle / What / ?

_____

c a / She's / pilot / .

_____

4 does / mom / What / do / your / ?

_____

d actor / He's / an / .

He's an actor.

4 **Look at activity 3. Complete the questions and answers.**

1 (your uncle) _____ _Where does_ _____ he _____ _work?_ _____

_____ _He works_ _____ in an animal hospital.

2 (your aunt) _____ she _____ ?

_____ in a plane.

3 (your dad) _____ he _____ ?

_____

4 (your mom) _____ she _____ ?

_____

5 **Write the name of a famous person. Then ask and answer with a friend.**

What does she do?   She's a singer.

Where does she work?   She works in theaters and studios.

6 **Read and number.**

What do you want to be?

1 I want to be a pilot.

3 I want to be a businesswoman.

5 I want to be a farmer.

2 I want to be a bus driver.

4 I want to be an actor.

7 **Look and write the questions and answers.**

1 What do you ___want to be?___

I ___want to be___ a doctor.

2 _____

_____

3 What do you _____ ?

I _____ a singer.

4 _____

_____

8 (About Me) **Answer the questions.**

1 Do you want to be a vet?

_____

2 Do you want to be a soccer player?

_____

3 Do you want to be a pilot?

_____

4 What do you want to be?

_____

Skills: *Writing*

9 **Read the paragraph and write the words.**

> ~~want to~~ math like office don't planes want to

What I want to be.

I ¹ ___want to___ be a pilot. I ² _____ seeing new things, and I like learning about new places. I'm good at ³ _____ . I ⁴ _____ want to work in an ⁵ _____ . I ⁶ _____ work on a plane and fly in the sky. I want to work with ⁷ _____ !

10 (About Me) **Answer the questions.**

1 What do you want to be?
   I want to be _____

2 What do you like doing?
   _____

3 What are you good at?
   _____

4 Where do you want to work?
   _____

5 Who/What do you want to work with?
   _____

11 (About Me) **Write about what you want to be.**

I want to be _____

_____

_____

_____

12 (About Me) **Ask and answer with a friend.**

What do you want to be?   I want to be a farmer.

13 Read and write the words.

Yes, please. ~~farmer~~ don't need to animals Should I help me

a Let's ask my uncle. He's a _farmer_. He has some on his farm.

b Hi, Uncle Jim. Can we have some rope and tires, please?

What for?

For the Adventure Playground.

OK, but can you _____ with the _____ first?

c _____ feed the hens?

OK!

_____. Lucas, can you give some water to the horse?

d Should I take the dog for a walk?

We _____, Anna. Let's look at the goats.

14 Look at activity 13. Circle the answers.

1 Lily's uncle is a _____ .
   a (farmer)   **b** rope   **c** tire

2 The ropes and tires are for _____ .
   a Lily's uncle   **b** the farm   **c** the Adventure Playground

3 Uncle Jim wants help with _____ .
   a the Adventure Playground **b** the animals **c** the farm

4 The water is for _____ .
   a the hens   **b** the horse   **c** the goats

5 They need to feed _____ .
   a the dog   **b** the horse   **c** the hens

15 Think **Read and check the activities that show the value: take care of pets and animals.**

1 ✓ love 2 ☐ borrow 3 ☐ give water

4 ☐ play with 5 ☐ take for a walk 6 ☐ do homework

7 ☐ feed 8 ☐ watch TV 9 ☐ brush hair

16 Think **Circle the words with the *cr* sound.**

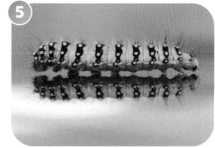

What kind of work is it?

1 **Match the kinds of work with the pictures.**

a outdoor work   **b** factory work   **c** transportation work   **d** store work

1 **b**

2

3

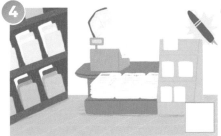
4

5

6

2 **Look and put the pictures in the correct order.**

a outdoor work   **b** factory work   **c** transportation work   **d** store work

1

_____ **d** _____

_____

_____

_____

2

_____

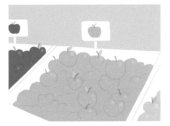

_____

_____

_____

Evaluation

1 **Find and circle the words. Then match.**

artistbusdriverbusinesswoman**nurse**businessmanactordoctorvetpilotsinger

2 Think **Look and complete the questions and answers.**

1

___What does your___ grandpa ___do___ ?

He's a ___nurse___ . _____ he work?

He works in a _____ .

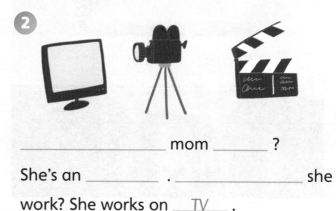

2

_____ mom _____ ?

She's an _____ . _____ she

work? She works on ___TV___ .

3 About Me **Complete the sentences about this unit.**

1 I can talk about _____ .

2 I can write about _____ .

3 My favorite part is _____ .

4 Puzzle **Guess what it is.**

This person can fly a helicopter.

Who is it? _____

Go to page 93 and write the answer.

4 Wild animals

1 **Look and check the correct words.**

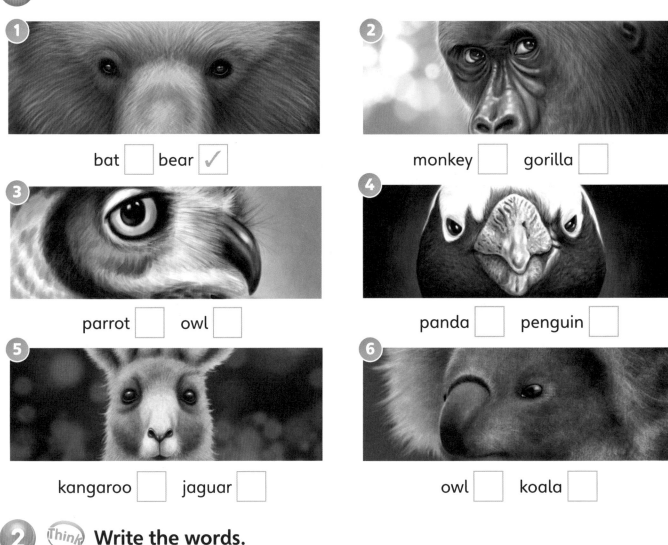

1
bat ☐ bear ✓

2
monkey ☐ gorilla ☐

3
parrot ☐ owl ☐

4
panda ☐ penguin ☐

5
kangaroo ☐ jaguar ☐

6
owl ☐ koala ☐

2 **Think** **Write the words.**

kangaroo   bat   penguin   ~~parrot~~   panda   jaguar

It can fly.	It has a long tail.	It's black and white.
parrot	_____	_____
_____	_____	_____

My picture dictionary → Go to page 88: Find and write the new words.

3 **Read and choose the correct words.**

1 Bears — are smaller than / are bigger than → gorillas.

2 Kangaroos — are slower than / are faster than — jaguars.

3 Koalas — are noisier than / are quieter than — bats.

4 Rabbits — are slower than / are faster than — penguins.

5 Parrots — are noisier than / are quieter than — snails.

4 **Look and complete the sentences. Use the words in the box.**

1 Gorillas are _____*bigger*_____ than jaguars.

2 Gorillas are _____ than koalas.

3 Koalas _____ jaguars.

4 Jaguars _____ gorillas.

big   small

5 Parrots are _____ than bats.

6 Bats are _____ than butterflies.

7 Butterflies _____ bats.

8 Bats _____ parrots.

noisy   quiet

5 (Think) **Read and circle the correct words.**

1 Are koalas **faster** / **slower** than gorillas?   Yes, they are.
2 Are owls **smaller** / **bigger** than pandas?   No, they aren't.
3 Are horses **taller** / **shorter** than gorillas?   No, they aren't.
4 Are parrots **noisier** / **quieter** than guinea pigs?   Yes, they are.
5 Are cats **longer** / **shorter** than jaguars?   No, they aren't.

6 **Look and use the words to complete the questions.**

fast / slow

tall / short

long / short

1 Are jaguars __faster than__ turtles?
Yes, they are.

2 Are turtles _____ jaguars?
Yes, they are.

3 Are kangaroos _____ penguins?
No, they aren't.

4 Are penguins _____ kangaroos?
No, they aren't.

5 Are dolphins _____ caterpillars?
Yes, they are.

6 Are caterpillars _____ dolphins?
Yes, they are.

7 **Complete the questions and write the answers.**

(~~tall~~   short   quiet   noisy)

1 Are you __taller than__ your friend?   _____
2 Are you _____ your friend?   _____
3 _____ your friend?   _____
4 _____ your friend?   _____

Skills: *Writing*

8 Read the paragraph and write the words.

> taller   spots   Africa   ~~long~~   leaves

My favorite animal

My favorite animal is the giraffe. Giraffes are very tall. They're brown and white, and they have a ¹ _long_ neck and ² _____ . They come from ³ _____ . They're wild animals, not pets. They eat ⁴ _____ . They're ⁵ _____ than a tree.

9 Answer the questions.

1 What's your favorite animal?

My favorite animal is _____

2 What does it look like?

_____

3 Where does it come from?

_____

4 What does it eat?

_____

5 Is it taller than a tree?

_____

10 Write about your favorite animal.

My favorite animal is _____

_____

_____

_____

11 Guess your friend's favorite animal.

It's smaller than a cat. It's slower than a guinea pig. It eats grass.

> Is it a turtle?

Yes, it is.

12 Read and number in order.

a

Grandpa, can you make an owl box for us?

Yes – you can help.

b

It's beautiful.

There you are! A house for an owl!

c

Where are the nails?

Here they are.

Can you pass them, please?

d

No, Anna. We need bigger boxes. Owls are bigger than other birds.

Are these owl boxes?

Let's make one.

e

Thank you. It's for the nature zone.

Wow! There are lots of boxes.

It's an owl town!

f

Are there bird boxes in your yard, Tom?

Yes, there are. But there aren't many.

1

13 Look at activity 12. Answer the questions.

1 What do they want to make?   _An owl box_

2 Why do they need to make one?   _____

3 Who helps them make it?   _____

4 What do they need to make it?   _____

5 What's an owl box?   _____

14 Look and check the pictures that show the value: take care of nature.

15 Look and write the words with the *fr* sound.

1 _____

2 _____

3 _____

What animal group is it?

1 Read the questions and write the words in the correct boxes.

frog panda ~~parrot~~ snake   fish amphibian ~~bird~~ mammal reptile

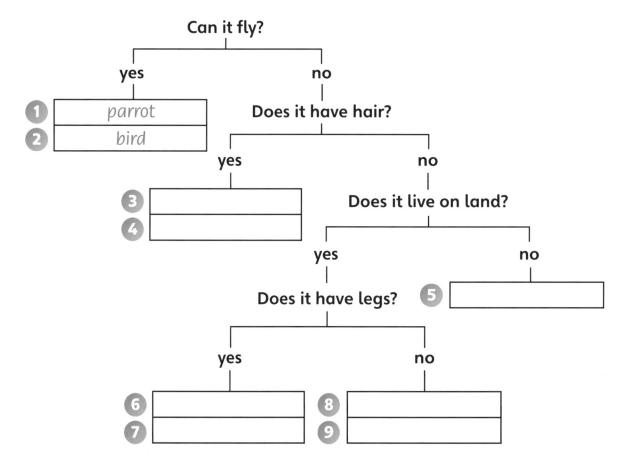

Can it fly?

yes
no

1 parrot
2 bird

Does it have hair?

yes
no

3
4

Does it live on land?

yes
no

Does it have legs?   **5**

yes
no

6   **8**
7   **9**

2 Look at activity 1. Write about a reptile, a bird, a mammal, and an amphibian.

1 *A snake is a reptile. It can't fly and it doesn't have hair. It lives on land.*

2 _____

3 _____

4 _____

Evaluation

1 (Think) **Find and circle ten animal words. Use the extra letters to answer the question.**

Where do gorillas come from?

A _ _ _ _ _

j	a	g	u	a	r	c	b	p	i
p	a	r	r	o	t	f	e	a	k
g	o	r	i	l	l	a	a	n	o
o	w	l	b	a	t	a	r	d	a
p	e	n	g	u	i	n	r	a	l
a	k	a	n	g	a	r	o	o	a

2 **Look and complete the sentences.**

~~big~~ small quiet fast

1 Gorillas are _____bigger_____ than koalas.

2 Owls are _____ than parrots.

3 Bats _____ kangaroos.

4 Jaguars _____ penguins.

3 (About Me) **Complete the sentences about this unit.**

1 I can talk about _____ .

2 I can write about _____ .

3 My favorite part is _____ .

4 (Puzzle) **Guess what it is.**

It's big and black and white. It eats leaves. What is it? _____

Go to page 93 and write the answer.

Review Units 3 and 4

1 Look and check the correct answers.

1 What do you want to be?

☑ **a** I want to be a teacher.

☐ **b** I want to be a businessman.

3 Do you want to be a soccer player?

☐ **a** Yes, I do.

☐ **b** No, I don't. I want to be a bus driver.

2 Do you want to be a singer?

☐ **a** Yes, I do.

☐ **b** No, I don't. I want to be a farmer.

4 What do you want to be?

☐ **a** I want to be an actor.

☐ **b** I want to be a businesswoman.

2 Read and complete the conversation.

Gemma: _What does your_ mom _____ ?

Paul: She's an _____ .
She likes drawing and painting.

Gemma: _____ she _____ ?

Paul: She works in a studio.

Gemma: Do you _____ an artist, too?

Paul: No, I don't. I like math.
I _____ a teacher.

Paul   Gemma

46

3 **Look and write the questions and answers.**

> short   long   small   ~~big~~

wallaby

kangaroo

bear

squirrel monkey

1 Are kangaroos ___*bigger than*___ wallabies? Yes, they are.

2 Are wallabies _____ kangaroos? Yes, _____ .

3 Are squirrel monkey tails _____ bear tails? No, _____ .

4 Are bear tails _____ squirrel monkey tails? No, _____ .

4 **Use the words to complete the questions. Then write answers.**

> ~~small~~   noisy   slow   big   fast

1 Are you ___*smaller than*___ a gorilla?   ___*Yes, I am.*___

2 Are you _____ a parrot?   _____

3 Are you _____ a jaguar?   _____

4 Are you _____ a koala?   _____

5 Are you _____ a turtle?   _____

5 Food and drink

1 Look and write the words.

pous
soup

ladsa
_____

zipza
_____

satap
_____

turgoy
_____

sciph
_____

ocioke
_____

tuns
_____

eat
_____

eofefc
_____

2 What do they want for lunch? Read and then write the words.

Tim: I want pizza for lunch!

Gina: I don't. I want pasta and salad.

Tim: I want salad, too. And yogurt. I like yogurt.

Gina: I want tea and a cookie, too.

Tim: I want tea, too.

Tim   Gina

pizza

My picture dictionary ➡ Go to page 89: Find and write the new words.

3 **Look and count. Then complete the sentences.**

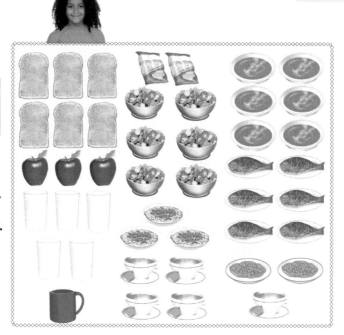

0	1–2	3–4	5–6
never	sometimes	usually	always

1 I _____usually_____ have tea for lunch.

2 I _____ have milk for lunch.

3 I _____ have fish for dinner.

4 I _____ have coffee for breakfast.

5 I _____ have apples for breakfast.

breakfast   lunch   dinner

4 **Look at activity 3. Then complete the sentences.**

1   She _____always has toast_____ for breakfast.

2    She _____ for lunch.

3    She _____ for dinner.

4 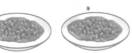   She _____ for dinner.

5   She _____ for breakfast.

5 **Complete the sentences.**

1 I _____ for breakfast.

2 I _____ for lunch.

3 I _____ for dinner.

6 (Think) **Look and complete the questions and answers.**

	Mia		
breakfast	✓✓✓ (tea/cup)	✓ (cookies)	✓✓ (cereal)
lunch	✓ (pizza)	✓✓✓ (salad)	✓✓ (soup)
dinner	✓✓ (fries)	✓✓✓ (meat)	✓ (carrots)

	never
✓	sometimes
✓✓	usually
✓✓✓	every day

1 _____How often do you have_____ cereal for breakfast?

I _____usually_____ have cereal for breakfast.

2 _____ salad for lunch?

I have salad for lunch _____ .

3 _____ meat for dinner?

I _____ meat for dinner _____ .

4 _____ carrots for dinner?

_____

5 _____ yogurt for breakfast?

_____

7 **Answer the questions.**

1 How often do you have cereal for breakfast? _____

2 How often do you have salad for lunch? _____

3 How often do you have fish for dinner? _____

Skills: *Writing*

8 **Make a lunch diary. Write what you eat and drink for lunch every day.**

cookies coffee chips nuts pasta pizza salad soup tea yogurt

Monday	Tuesday	Wednesday	Thursday	Friday

9 **Look at activity 8. Answer the questions.**

1 What do you usually have for lunch? _____

2 What do you sometimes have for lunch? _____

3 What do you eat or drink every day for lunch? _____

4 What do you never have for lunch? _____

5 Do you have a healthy lunch? _____

10 **Write about what you eat for lunch.**

I usually eat _____

_____

_____

_____

_____

11 **Ask and answer with a friend.**

What do you eat for lunch?

I usually have rice and beans. Sometimes I drink milk.

12 Read and match.

1 Can I have two, please?　2 ~~$15! That's a lot of money.~~
3 Let's wash our hands first.　4 How about selling fruit?

13 Look at activity 12. Write *yes* or *no*.

1 They need to get a lot of money. _____yes_____

2 Lucas's dad gives them money to buy fruit. _____

3 Washing your hands before touching food is a good idea. _____

4 The fruit salad costs two dollars. _____

5 Lucas's grandma sells fruit salad. _____

14 Look and check the pictures that show the value: be clean around food.

1
a

b ✓

2
a

b

3
a

b

15 Circle the words with the *ar* sound.

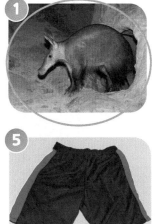

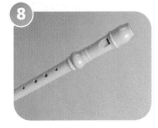

Where does water come from?

1 **Look and write.**

~~cloud~~   glacier   mountain   rain   river   ocean   spring   well

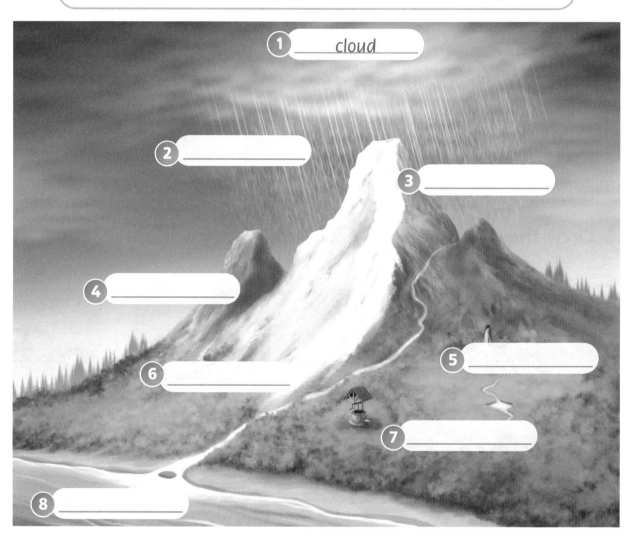

1 _____cloud_____

2 _____

3 _____

4 _____

5 _____

6 _____

7 _____

8 _____

2 **Complete the sentences about water.**

1 Water comes from c _louds____ and r_____ .

2 Some people drink water from a w_____ or a s_____ .

3 We can see a g_____ in the mountains.

4 A r_____ goes to the o_____ .

Evaluation

1 **Look and match.**

1 yogurt	h	**2** chips
3 pasta		**4** salad
5 tea		**6** coffee
7 nuts		**8** pizza
9 soup		**10** cookie

a
b
c
d
e
f
g
h
i
j

2 **Look and write.**

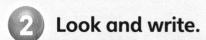

	Monday	Tuesday	Wednesday	Thursday	Friday
	cake	cake	chips	cake	cake
Emile	nuts	nuts	cake	nuts	coffee

1 How often does Emile have chips? _____Sometimes._____

2 How often does he have cake? _____

3 How often does he have pizza? _____

4 How often does he have nuts? _____

5 How often does he have coffee? _____

3 (About Me) **Complete the sentences about this unit.**

1 I can talk about _____ .

2 I can write about _____ .

3 My favorite part is _____ .

4 (Puzzle) **Guess what it is.**

It's a drink. It's dark brown. It's usually hot. It's not tea. What is it?

_____

Go to page 93 and write the answer.

6 Health matters

1 Look and write the words.

backache
cold
cough
earache
headache
~~sore throat~~
stomachache
temperature
toothache

1 _sore throat_   2 _____   3 _____   4 _____

5 _____   6 _____   7 _____   8 _____   9 _____

2 Look and complete the sentences.

1 Dan has a
stomachache .

2 Grace has a
_____ .

3 Ann has a
_____ .

4 May has a
_____ .

5 Tony has a
_____ .

Ann   Tony   Grace   May   Dan

My picture dictionary Go to page 90: Find and write the new words.

3 Look and write.

What's the ____matter____ , Kelly?

I have a ____cold____ , an ____earache____ , and a _____ .

What's the _____ , Bill?

I have a _____ , a _____ _____ ,

and a _____ .

_____ , Sue?

I have an _____ , a _____ , and

a _____ .

4 Think! Look at activity 3. Write the words.

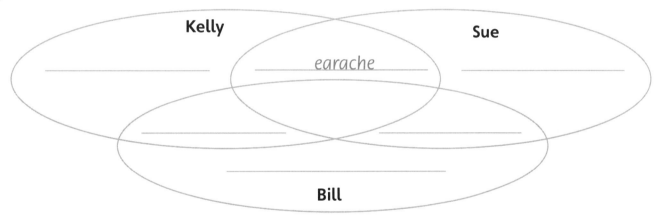

Kelly   Sue

_____   ____earache____   _____

_____   _____

_____

Bill

5 Look and write the questions and answers.

1 What's the ____matter____ ?

I have _____ ____an earache____ .

2 What's the _____ ?

I have _____ .

3 What's the _____ ?

I have _____ .

4 _____ ?

_____

6 **Complete the questions and say why you can't.**

1. _Can you_ go kayaking today?
   No, I _can't_ . I have a _temperature_ .

2. _____ go snowboarding today?
   No, I _____ . I have a _____ .

3. _____ go to the museum today?
   _____ .

4. _____ play soccer today?
   _____ .

5. _____ go swimming today?
   _____ .

7 (About Me) **Complete the sentences. Use the words in the box.**

> a cold   an earache   ~~a backache~~   a temperature

1. Can you go bowling today?
   No, _____I can't_____ .
   _____I have a backache_____ .

2. Can you go kayaking today?
   No, _____ .
   _____ .

3. Can you go to the movies tonight?
   No, _____ .
   _____ .

4. Can you go swimming tomorrow?
   No, _____ .
   _____ .

Skills: *Writing*

8 **Read and write the words.**

~~favorite~~   wash   yogurt   lunch   need

Apple and nut salad is my ¹___*favorite*___ salad. It's healthy because apples and nuts are good for you. Sometimes I have this salad for ²_____ .

- You ³_____ apples, nuts, cheese, yogurt, and carrots.
- ⁴_____ the fruits and vegetables. Cut the apples, carrots, and cheese.
- Add some ⁵_____ .

9 (About Me) **Answer the questions.**

1 What's your favorite healthy food or drink?

My favorite healthy _____

2 Why is it healthy?

_____

3 What do you need to make it?

_____

4 How do you make it?

_____

5 How often do you eat / drink it?

_____

10 (About Me) **Write a recipe for your favorite healthy food or drink.**

_____

_____

_____

_____

11 (About Me) **Ask and answer with a friend.**

What's your favorite healthy food or drink?

My favorite healthy food is salad.

12 Read and write the words.

headache   ~~competition~~   leg hurts   very good   OK now

It's a _competition_!

Go, Chris!

Oh, dear!

Are you OK, Chris?

Yes, I think so. My _____ , but I'm OK. Don't worry.

Do you have a _____ , Chris?

No, I'm _____ .

But where's your skateboard?

Good job, Max!

Sorry, Chris!

That's OK! I'm good at skateboarding, but Max is _____ !

13 Look at activity 12. Circle the correct words.

1 Chris has a skateboarding **club** / (**competition**) / **team**.
2 Chris's **leg** / **head** / **ear** hurts.
3 Chris says he doesn't have a **backache** / **stomachache** / **headache**.
4 Max is **really bad** / **OK** / **really good** at skateboarding.
5 **Chris** / **Tom** / **Lily** is a good sport.

14 Look and check the pictures that show the value: be a good sport.

15 Connect the words with the *sp* sound.

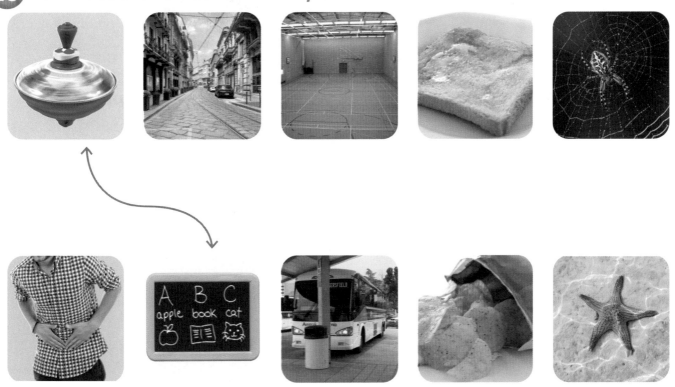

What can we use plants for?

1 **Read and match.**

1   We can use trees for fuel.   `c`

2   We can use plants to give us cereal. ☐

3   We can use the fruit from plants for medicine. ☐

4   We can use the wood from trees to give us shelter. ☐

5   We can use plants to make fabric. ☐

2 **Draw a plant. Then write three ways we can use your plant.**

1 _____

_____

_____

2 _____

_____

3 _____

_____

Evaluation

1 **Think** **Look and then complete the sentences.**

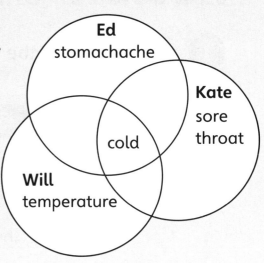

1 _What's the matter_ with Will?

   He has a _cold_ and a _____ .

2 _____ Ed?

   He has a _____ and a _____ .

3 _____ Kate?

   _____ and a _____ .

Ed
stomachache

Kate
sore throat

cold

Will
temperature

2 **Read and then complete the answers.**

1 Can you go to the movies today?

> My head hurts.
> No, I _can't_ . I have a _headache_ .

2 Can you go to the café tonight?

> My tooth hurts.
> No, I _____ . I have a _____ .

3 Can you play basketball this afternoon?

> My back hurts.
> _____

3   **Complete the sentences about this unit.**

1 I can talk about _____ .

2 I can write about _____ .

3 My favorite part is _____ .

4   **Guess what it is.**

Eating a lot of food can give you

a _____ . What is it?

Go to page 93 and write the answer.

Review Units 5 and 6

1 (Think) **Complete the sentences.**

breakfast / me

lunch / Kim

X = never

✓ = sometimes

✓✓ = usually

✓✓✓ = always

1 _____Sometimes_____ she _____has_____ soup for lunch.

2 I _____ yogurt for breakfast.

3 She _____ rice for lunch.

4 I _____ tea for breakfast.

5 _____ she _____ a sandwich for lunch.

6 _____ I _____ toast for breakfast.

2 (Think) **Read and then write the words.**

Leo and Carol usually have pizza for lunch and Billy usually has fish. Sometimes Leo has a sandwich and sometimes Billy and Carol have salad. Leo and Billy usually have chips and Carol has yogurt. Carol, Billy, and Leo always drink tea for lunch.

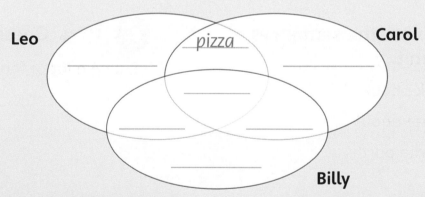

Leo   *pizza*   **Carol**

Billy

3 (About Me) **Answer the questions.**

1 What do you always have for breakfast? _____

2 What do you usually have for lunch? _____

3 What do you sometimes have for dinner? _____

4 What do you never have for dinner? _____

4 (Think) **Find the letters and write the words. Then match.**

a	b	c	d	e	f	g	h	i	j	k	l	m
■	▼	♦	✖	●	✚	★	◗	❙	⦂	↓	♥	✳

n	o	p	q	r	s	t	u	v	w	x	y	z
()	▲	⬟	◖	▲	/	▬	↑	❀	◣	◆	⬭	⚡

1 ♦ ▲ ↑ ★ ◗
_c_ _o_ _u_ _g_ _h_

2 ◗ ● ■ ✖ ■ ♦ ◗ ●
_ _ _ _ _ _ _ _

3 ▬ ● ✳ ⬟ ● ● ▲ ■ ▬ ↑ ▲ ●
_ _ _ _ _ _ _ _ _ _ _ _

4 ▬ ▲ ▲ ▬ ✖ ◗ ■ ♦ ◗ ●
_ _ _ _ _ _ _ _ _ _

5 ♦ ▲ ♥ ✖
_ _ _ _

6 / ▲ ▲ ●   ▬ ◖ ▲ ▲ ▬
_ _ _ _   _ _ _ _ _ _

7 ▼ ■ ♦ ↓ ■ ♦ ◗ ●
_ _ _ _ _ _ _ _

8 / ▬ ▲ ✳ ■ ♦ ◗ ■ ♦ ◗ ●
_ _ _ _ _ _ _ _ _ _ _

9 ● ■ ▲ ■ ♦ ◗ ●
_ _ _ _ _ _ _

 1

5 **Read and complete the answers.**

Oh, dear   ~~I think so~~   I don't think so   Oh, good   Don't worry

1 **A:** Are you OK?
   B: Yes, _I think so_ .
   A: _____ .
   B: _____ !

2 **A:** Are you OK?
   B: No, _____ . I have
      an earache.
   A: _____ !

1 Look and number.

1 ~~attic~~
2 basement
3 stairs
4 elevator
5 roof
6 first floor
7 second floor
8 third floor
9 fourth floor
10 garage

2 Think **Look at activity 1. Write the words.**

1 There's a kite on the ___roof___ .

2 There's a cat in the _____ .

3 There's a car in the _____ .

4 There's a skateboard on the _____ .

5 There's a man on the _____ _____ .

6 There's a woman on the _____ _____ .

My picture dictionary Go to page 91: Find and write the new words.

3 **Put the words in order. Then write the number.**

1 you / Where / morning / yesterday / were / ?

Where were you yesterday morning?

the / was / I / kitchen / in / .

I was in the kitchen.

2 were / afternoon / you / Where / yesterday / ?

_____

third / on / I / the / was / floor / .

_____

3 yesterday / you / evening / were / Where / ?

_____

in / I / room / the / was / living / .

_____

4 morning / were / yesterday / Where / you / ?

_____

was / I / in / garage / the / .

_____

5 night / were / you / last / Where / ?

_____

bedroom / floor / I / in / my / on / the / fourth / was / .

_____

4 (About Me) **Answer the questions.**

1 Where were you yesterday morning?

_____

2 Where were you yesterday afternoon?

_____

3 Where were you yesterday evening?

_____

4 Where were you last night?

_____

5 (Think) **Look and check *Yes, I was* or *No, I wasn't*.**

	Yes, I was.	No, I wasn't.
1 Were you at the sports field yesterday morning?	☐	✓
2 Were you at the beach yesterday morning?	☐	☐
3 Were you at a restaurant yesterday afternoon?	☐	☐
4 Were you at home last night?	☐	☐
5 Were you at the movies yesterday evening?	☐	☐

10 o'clock   *at the beach*

3 o'clock   *at the shopping mall*

6 o'clock   *at the sports field*

11 o'clock   *at home*

6 **Look and write.**

yesterday morning	yesterday afternoon	yesterday evening	last night

1 _Were you_ at the sports center yesterday evening?   Yes, _I was_ .

2 _____ at home yesterday afternoon?   No, _____ .

3 _____ at school yesterday afternoon?   Yes, _____ .

4 _____ in your bedroom yesterday morning?   Yes, _____ .

5 _____ at the movies last night?   No, _____ .

7 (About Me) **Answer the questions.**

1 Were you at school yesterday morning? _____

2 Were you at the library yesterday afternoon? _____

3 Were you on the bus yesterday evening? _____

4 Were you at a restaurant last night? _____

Skills: *Writing*

8 Read the text. Circle the answers to the questions.

On Saturday morning, I was (at the park) with my dog. Then I was at a café at lunchtime. In the afternoon, I was at the sports center. It was exciting. I love playing basketball! In the evening, I was at the movie theater.

1 Where were you in the morning?
2 Where were you at lunchtime?
3 Where were you in the afternoon?
4 Where were you in the evening?

9 (About Me) Look at activity 8. Choose a day. Answer the questions for you.

Day: _____

1 _____

2 _____

3 _____

4 _____

10 (About Me) Write about your day.

_____

_____

_____

_____

_____

_____

11 (About Me) Ask and answer with a friend.

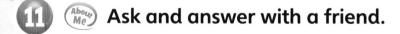

Where were you in the morning?   I was at school.

12 Read and number in order.

a
No! It's a turtle!
It looks like my cousin Kim's turtle!
Let's call and ask her.

b
Oh, Speedy! Thank you so much!
What can we give you for a reward?
LOST TURTLE REWARD

c
Hello. I think we've got your turtle.
Great! Where was he?
He was in my garage!

d
Here's my old bike. Oh, dear!
Look. Is that a helmet?
Week 7 We need bikes and helmets.
1

e
Do you have an old bike?
Yes, I do!
A helmet too, please!

f
Hello?
Hello. It's Lily. Is Kim there, please?
Yes, she is. Just a minute.

13 Look at activity 12. Answer the questions.

1 Who has an old bike? _____Lily_____

2 Is it a helmet or a turtle? _____

3 Whose turtle is it? _____

4 Where was the turtle? _____

5 What's the turtle's name? _____

14 Look and check the pictures that show the value: take care of your possessions.

15 Color the words with the letters *ck*.

Which materials were buildings made of?

1 **Look and match.**

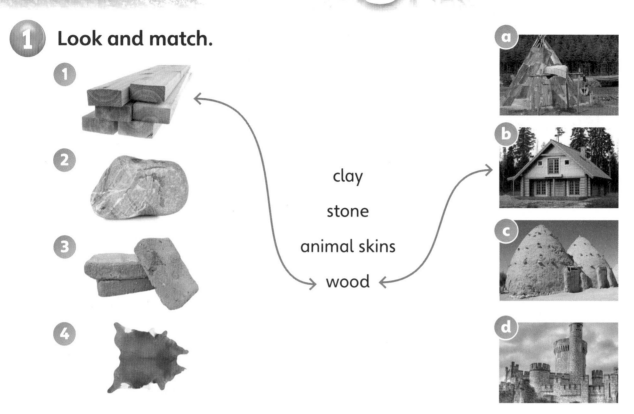

1

2

3

4

clay

stone

animal skins

wood

a

b

c

d

2 **Draw your house. Then write about the old building and your house.**

1   The old building was made of _____ *stone* _____ .

My house is made of _____ .

2   The old building is _____ than my house.

3   The old building has _____ floors.

My house has _____ floors.

4   I don't think the old building has

a _____ .

5   My house has a _____ .

Old stone castle.

My house.

Evaluation

1 **Do the word puzzle.**

Across →

1 You can put a car and a bicycle here.
2 They're slower than the elevator.
4 It's above the fourth floor and below the roof.
5 It's between the second floor and the attic.
7 It's below the first floor.
8 It's above the basement.

Down ↓

3 It's below the third floor.
6 It's above the attic.

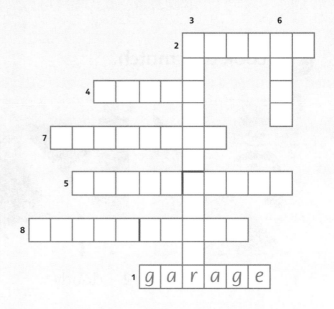

2 **Complete the questions and answers.**

1 **Mark:** Where ___*were you*___ yesterday morning?
2 **Eva:** _____ at the beach.
3 **Mark:** Where were you in the afternoon?
4 **Eva:** _____ at the movies.
5 **Mark:** _____ at a restaurant in the evening?
6 **Eva:** No, _____ . I was at home.

> I was
> I was
> I wasn't
> ~~were you~~
> Were you

3 **Complete the sentences about this unit.**

1 I can talk about _____ .
2 I can write about _____ .
3 My favorite part is _____ .

4 **Guess what it is.**

It's faster than the stairs.

What is it? _____

Go to page 93 and write the answer.

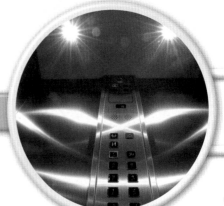

1 Look and match.

1 snowy `a` **2** cloudy ☐ **3** windy ☐ **4** sunny ☐

  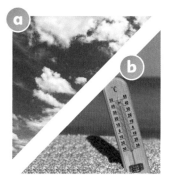 

5 foggy ☐ **6** cold ☐ **7** hot ☐ **8** rainy ☐

2 Write the words.

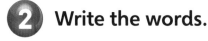

~~cold~~   hot   warm

1 _____cold_____   **2** _____   **3** _____

My picture dictionary Go to page 92: Find and write the new words.

3 Look and write.

1

Yesterday at 10:00.

What was the weather like _yesterday morning_ ?

It was warm and rainy.

2

Yesterday at 15:00.

_____ the weather like _____ ?

_____ and _____ .

3

Yesterday at 19:00.

_____ the weather like _____ ?

_____

4

Yesterday at 23:00.

_____ the weather like _____ ?

_____ and _____ .

5

Today.

_____ ?

_____

4 (About Me) Answer the questions.

1 What was the weather like yesterday morning?

_____

2 What was the weather like last night?

_____

3 What's the weather like today?

_____

4 What's your favorite weather?

_____

5 Think **Read and match. Then write the days.**

1 Was it cold and foggy on Tuesday?
No, it wasn't. It was warm and windy.

_____

2 Was it hot and rainy on Thursday?
No, it wasn't. It was cold and snowy.

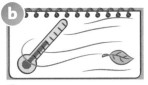
_____Tuesday_____

3 Was it hot and sunny on Friday?
Yes, it was.

_____

4 Was it cold and cloudy on Wednesday?
No, it wasn't. It was hot and rainy.

_____

5 Was it hot and cloudy on Monday?
No, it wasn't. It was cold and cloudy.

_____

6 **Look and complete the questions and answers.**

| Tuesday | Thursday | Saturday | Sunday |

1 _____Was it_____ warm and rainy on Tuesday?

_____Yes, it was._____

2 _____ cold and snowy on Thursday?

_____

3 _____ hot and windy on Saturday?

No, it wasn't. It was _____ and _____ .

4 _____ cold and cloudy on Sunday?

_____

Skills: *Writing*

7 **Read about Jane's favorite festival and answer the questions.**

On Sunday I was at the Bristol hot-air balloon festival with my family.
The balloon festival's every August. The weather is usually hot and sunny.
The festival's really big, and there are lots of beautiful hot-air balloons.
You can fly in a hot-air balloon. I like taking photographs of the balloons.
They're fantastic!

1 What's Jane's favorite festival?

Jane's favorite festival is _____

2 When is it?

_____

3 What's the weather like?

_____

4 What can you see there?

_____

5 What can you do at the festival?

_____

8 (About Me) **Answer the questions for you.**

1 _____

2 _____

3 _____

4 _____

5 _____

9 (About Me) **Write about your favorite festival.**

My favorite festival _____

_____

_____

10 (About Me) **Ask and answer with a friend.**

What's your favorite festival?　　　The Songkran water festival.

11 Read and match.

1 thank you for your hard work!
2 What time does the party start?
3 ~~Please come to the opening party on Saturday at four o'clock.~~
4 The Adventure Playground is now open!

Adventure Playground

Good job, everyone!
Our Adventure Playground is ready!

3

It's Saturday today!

At four o'clock.

Adventure Playground

Good job, everyone!
Our Adventure Playground is ready!
Please come to the opening party
on Saturday at four o' clock.

Hurry up, we're late!

Adventure Playground

Welcome, everyone, and _____!

I want to be on TV!

_____!

12 Look at activity 11. Write yes or no.

1 The Adventure Playground is ready.   _yes_

2 The party's on Sunday.   _____

3 The party starts at five o'clock.   _____

4 Tom says thank you.   _____

5 Anna wants to be on TV.   _____

13 Look and check the pictures that show the value: work hard and try your best.

1

2  ✓

3

4

5

6

14 Look and write the words with the *nd* sound.

1 _____sand_____

2 _____

3 _____

4 _____

a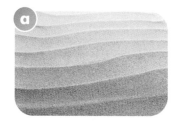

b

c

d

e

f

g

h

What's the weather like around the world?

1 🄣🄗🄘🄝🄚 **Put the letters in order. Then match and write.**

1 There's a **rizlbazd** with lots of snow. | e | _blizzard_
2 It's very cloudy, and there's a **rsairtnmo**. | ☐ | _____
3 There's a **uihrrance** above the ocean. | ☐ | _____
4 There's a **rnootda**. It looks like a cone. | ☐ | _____
5 There's **hteundr** and **ghnlintig**. | ☐ | _____ and _____

a b c d e

2 **What's the weather like in Adventure Land? Draw and write.**

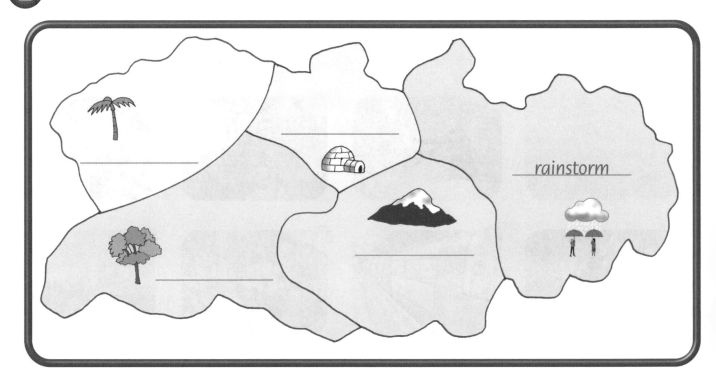

rainstorm

Evaluation

 1 (Think) **Look and write.**

yesterday morning	yesterday afternoon	yesterday evening	last night

it was	
it was	
It was	
it wasn't	
Was it	
Was it	
~~What was~~	
yesterday evening	
~~yesterday morning~~	
yesterday afternoon	
Was it	

1 ___What was___ the weather like _yesterday morning_ ?

_____ cold and foggy.

2 _____ warm and windy last night?

No, _____ . It was cold and snowy.

3 _____ warm and windy _____ ? Yes, _____ .

4 _____ cold and rainy _____ ? Yes, _____ .

2 (About Me) **Complete the sentences about this unit.**

1 I can talk about _____ .

2 I can write about _____ .

3 My favorite part is _____ .

3 (Puzzle) **Guess what it is.**

You need an umbrella for this weather. What is it?

_____

Go to page 93 and write the answer.

81

Review   Units 7 and 8

1 (Think) **Look and write.**

1 Where ___were you___ yesterday?

___I was___ at home.

2 Where _____ yesterday morning?

_____ in the _____ .

3 Where _____ yesterday afternoon?

_____ in the _____ .

4 Where _____ yesterday evening?

_____ in the _____ .

5 _____ last night?

_____ in my _____ .

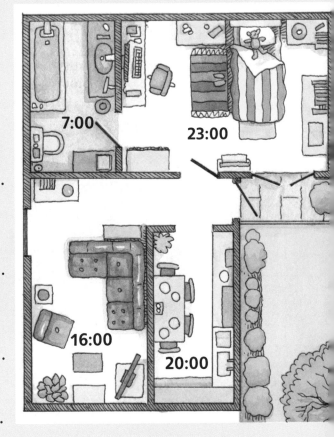

7:00   23:00

16:00   20:00

2 **Look and write.**

1 ___Were you___ at the shopping mall in the afternoon?

___Yes, I was.___

2 _____ at the movie theater yesterday afternoon?

_____

3 _____ at home yesterday morning?

_____

3 (About Me) **Answer the questions.**

1 Where were you yesterday morning? _____

2 Where were you yesterday afternoon? _____

3 Where were you yesterday evening? _____

4 Where were you last night? _____

Look and write.

yesterday   today

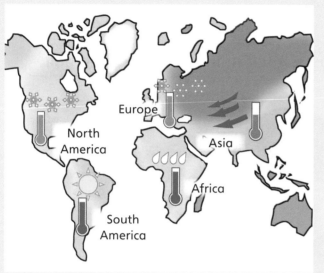   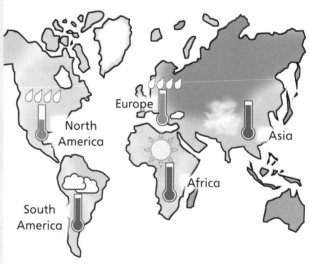

1 _____What's_____ the weather like in Africa today?

_It's hot and sunny._____

2 _____What was_____ the weather like in Africa yesterday?

_It was hot and rainy._____

3 _____ the weather like in North America today?

_____

4 _____ the weather like in North America yesterday?

_____

5 _____ the weather like in Asia today?

_____

6 _____ the weather like in Asia yesterday?

_____

7 _____ the weather like in South America today?

_____

8 _____ the weather like in South America yesterday?

_____

Welcome back!

dark hair   straight hair   glasses   fair hair   ~~curly hair~~   red hair

curly hair

1 Fun sports

ice-skating   sailing   skiing   kayaking   skateboarding   fishing
~~bowling~~   mountain biking   snowboarding

bowling

traffic light   museum   hotel   subway station   shopping mall
bus station   crosswalk   square   ~~bank~~   restaurant

bank

3 At work

vet ~~actor~~ singer doctor pilot businesswoman
artist bus driver nurse businessman

actor

4 Wild animals

parrot   gorilla   owl   koala   panda   jaguar   ~~bat~~   penguin   kangaroo   bear

bat

5 Food and drink

cookie pizza pasta chips nuts coffee soup tea salad yogurt

cookie

_____

_____

_____

_____

_____

_____

_____

_____

_____

6 Health matters

temperature ~~backache~~ cold headache cough
stomachache sore throat earache toothache

backache

7 Buildings

stairs   basement   fourth floor   roof   ~~attic~~   third floor
elevator   garage   second floor   first floor

attic

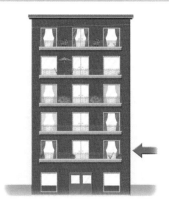

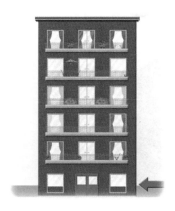

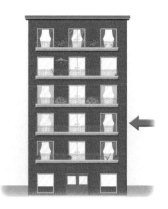

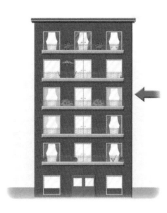

8 Weather

foggy   snowy   hot   rainy   warm   windy   ~~cold~~   cloudy   sunny

cold

_____

_____

_____

_____

_____

_____

_____

_____

Puzzle

Across →

3 **(Unit 4)** It's big and black and white. It eats leaves. What is it?

4 **(Welcome back!)** Hair that's not straight. What is it?

5 **(Unit 6)** Eating a lot of food can give you a … What is it?

7 **(Unit 1)** You need water and wind to do this sport. What is it?

8 **(Unit 7)** It's faster than the stairs. What is it?

Down ↓

1 **(Unit 8)** You need an umbrella for this weather. What is it?

2 **(Unit 2)** You stop when it's red. You go when it's green. What is it? (two words)

3 **(Unit 3)** This person can fly a helicopter. Who is it?

6 **(Unit 5)** It's a drink. It's dark brown. It's usually hot. It's not tea. What is it?

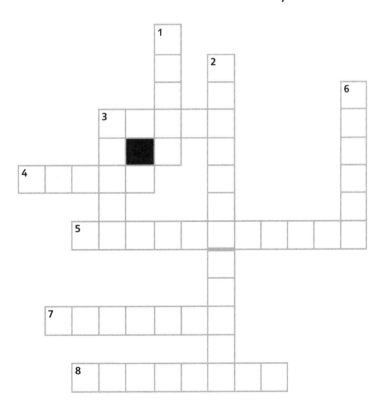

Story fun

1 **Match the objects to the words. Then match the words to the story units they come from.**

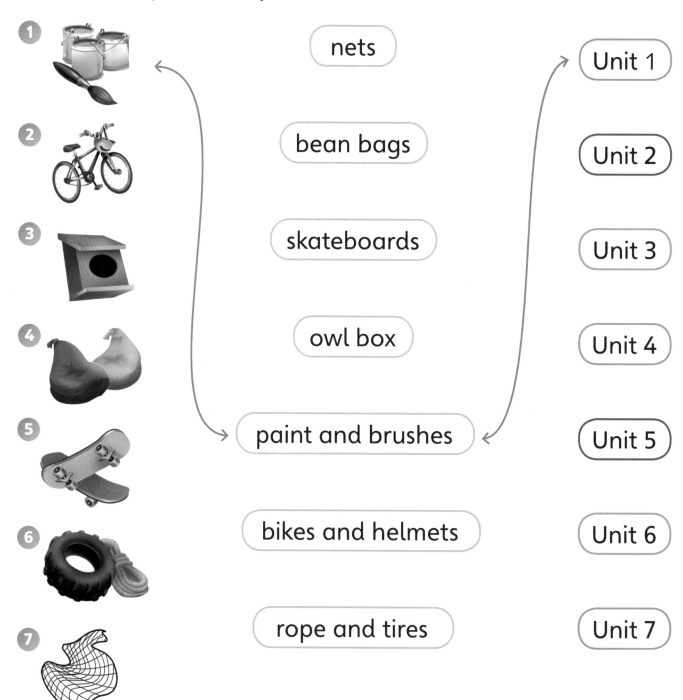

1
2
3
4
5
6
7

nets

bean bags

skateboards

owl box

paint and brushes

bikes and helmets

rope and tires

Unit 1

Unit 2

Unit 3

Unit 4

Unit 5

Unit 6

Unit 7

2 Look and find the missing people and objects. Write the numbers in the boxes.